Finding "Washoku"

~Japanese Food Culture~

Study Group of Japanese Food Culture and Educational Program

Preface

"*Washoku*", traditional Japanese cuisine, was registered in the UNESCO Representative List of the Intangible Cultural Heritage of Humanity in December 2013.

The Japanese Ministry of Agriculture, Forestry and Fisheries cited the following four points as the characteristics of "*Washoku*".

1) Respect for nature blessed with fresh seasonal ingredients from the sea, the mountains, and the countryside and the use of natural resources.
2) Nutritionally well-balanced and healthy diet.
3) Presentation of the natural beauties and the changes of four seasons.
4) Closely connected to annual events like New Year's Day.

"*Washoku*" is becoming very popular in the world. An increasing number of foreign tourists must have tried Japanese food and they would like to enjoy it again.

This book is dedicated to those who live in other countries. It introduces the characteristics and the heart of Japanese food culture with pleasant illustrations for help. We focus not only on the special foods and their meaning in some seasonal festivals in Japan but on the ingredients supporting Japanese food culture.

We hope our readers will cultivate a better understanding of Japanese food culture and enjoy more "*Washoku*".

Nara Women's University
Kimiko Ohtani, Ph.D.

Contents

Heart of "*Washoku*" 7
Heart of "*Omotenashi*"
Basic manners to enjoy "*Washoku*"
Heart of "*Shojin-ryori*"
Heart of "*Kaiseki-ryori*"

Seasonal Events and Foods 12
New Year's Day on January 1
"*Jinjitsu no Sekku*" on January 7
"*Setsubun*" on February 3
"*Joushi no Sekku*" on March 3
"*Tango no Sekku*" on May 5
"*Shichiseki no Sekku*" on July 7
"*Chouyou no Sekku*" on September 9
"*Oomisoka*" on December 31

Arrangement of "*Washoku*" 21
Two Basic Principles of "*Washoku*"
Expression of the Sense of Seasons
Various Cutting Techniques with Kitchen Knives

Foods add color to "*Washoku*" 25

Staple Food of "*Washoku*": Rice

Leading Food of "*Washoku*": Fish

Excellent Supporter of "*Washoku*": Vegetables

Accent of "*Washoku*": Soybean

Accent of "*Washoku*": *Tsukemono*

Partner of "*Washoku*": *Cha*

Wagashi

Sake

Foods enhancing the taste of "*Washoku*" 34

Water

Dashi

Salt

Miso and *Shoyu*

Mirin

References ………………………40

Heart of "*Washoku*"

Heart of *"Omotenashi"*

"Omotenashi" is a traditional Japanese way of hospitality with utmost dedication and exquisite manners treasuring every meeting as it will never recur.

In addition to good manners, you can expect refined use of language expressions and a gentle mien of the restaurant staff. We see the heart of *"Omotenashi"* expressed not only in the elegantly cooked dishes, but anywhere in the restaurant such as the entrance purified by water, a well-cared garden, elaborately designed rooms and decorated interiors depending on the season. The heart of *"Omotenashi"* provides guests with comfort and relaxation time.

And it is the Japanese custom to say *"Itadakimasu"* at the beginning of the meal and *"Gochisousama"* at the end of it. These two words are the expressions to say "thank you" to all for the food we are going to partake of.

Basic manners to enjoy "*Washoku*"

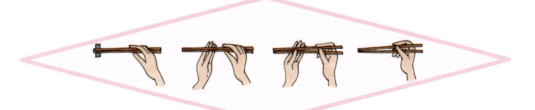

Manners to pick up "*Hashi*"

It is recommended to respond to the heart of "*Omotenashi*" by showing your appreciation to the delicious dishes cooked and elegantly served. Good manners are means to express your appreciation.

One of the characteristics of Japanese food culture is to use "*Hashi* (箸: chopsticks)" when eating. And we have to use "*Hashi*" in good manners and be careful of so called bad manners as "*Kiraibashi* (嫌い箸)" shown below.

Let's enjoy "*Washoku*" in elegant manners.

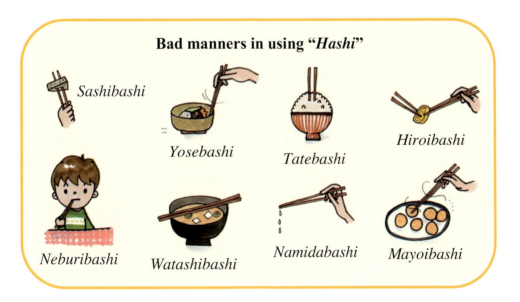

Heart of "*Shojin-ryori* (*Zen* vegetalian dishes)"

You must value rice and vegetables just as you take good care of your own eyes.

"*Tenzokyoukun*"

"*Shojin-ryori* (精進料理)" was originally prepared as vegetarian dishes harmonizing with rules of bringing out the best in the inherent qualities of ingredients.

Dogen (1200-1253), *Zen* (禅) master of *Soto* sect, taught that the food plays important roles in mental and spiritual development of both cooks and diners. The food should be prepared with respect and gratitude for ingredients without wasting the parts that are thrown away in ordinary cooking. It should be eaten with modest heart. He showed "*Sanshin* (三心)" and "*Santoku* (三徳)" as the most important attitude to cook. "*Sanshin*" are "*Kishin* (喜心: to feel pleasure to be able to cook)", "*Roushin* (老心: to cook by putting yourself in the place of diners)" and "*Daishin* (大心: to cook on the basic principles without forgetting your first resolution)". "*Santoku*" are "*Kyounan* (軽軟: to cook with the respect for the inherent qualities of ingredients)", "*Jouketsu* (浄潔: to keep clean and hygienic)" and "*Nyohousa* (如法作: to cook according to the basic principles)".

Heart of "*Kaiseki-ryori*"

There is the concept of "*Ichigo ichie* (一期一会)", once-in-a-lifetime-opportunity, in "*Cha-do* (茶道: literally the way of tea)". The host or hostess should do his or her best to treat guests throughout the tea ceremony as today will never occur again.

The tea ceremony involves not only the manners of tea but also the *Zen* spirit, "*Wabi* (侘び: austere refinement)", rationality and consideration for others. The basic philosophy of "*Cha-do*" is shown in the words, "*Wa* (和: harmony)", "*Kei* (敬: respect each other)", "*Sei* (清: purify your surroundings and your spirit)" and "*Jaku* (寂: maintain a spirit of quietness)".

"*Kaiseki-ryori* (懐石料理)" is a light meal to enjoy before the bowl of "*Koicha* (濃茶)", a thick powdered green tea. This is because "*Koicha*" is very heavy for the empty stomach. "*Kaiseki-ryori*" should be served with best hospitality in the quiet "*Cha-shitsu* (茶室: a traditional Japanese tea room)".

"*Cha-do*" treasures the sense of seasons not only in the ingredients of "*Kaiseki-ryori*" but in the design of "*Wagashi* (*cf*. p.32)" served before "*Koicha*". The alcove called "*Tokonoma* (床の間)" is also important in "*Cha-do*" and should be arranged carefully according to this sense of seasons.

Seasonal Events and Foods

New Year's Day on January 1

Zouni *Osechi-ryori* *Tosoki*

The Japanese prepare special dishes called "*Osechi-ryori* (お節料理)" arranged beautifully in lacquer boxes for the New Year's Day in order to welcome "*Toshigami* (歳神: a *Shinto* God of the incoming year)". We pray to God for a rich harvest and health for the year. Each delicacy packed in the "*Osechi-ryori*" has its own meaning associated with good health, good harvest, happiness, prosperity or long life coming from the color or implications of the delicacy.

"*Zouni* (雑煮)" is also an essential soup dish, which contains "*Mochi* (餅: rice cakes)" together with other seasonal ingredients.

"*Osechi-ryori*" and "*Zouni*" are believed to be important ritual foods to eat with "*Toshigami*", which is called "*Shinjin-kyoushoku* (神人供食)". We use special chopsticks for the New Year celebrations called "*Iwaibashi* (祝箸)" made of willow with two sides, one for us and the other for God.

And New Year's special "*Sake* (酒: rice wine)" called "*Otoso* (お屠蘇)", which is made by immersing "*Tososan* (屠蘇散: blend of several types of herbs)" in "*Mirin* (*cf.* p.39)", is usually served by a set of "*Sake*" utensils called "*Tosoki* (屠蘇器)" in order to get rid of evil spirits and pray for the perfect health of the year.

"*Jinjitsu no Sekku*" on January 7

The *Edo* Shogunate designated representative five seasonal festivals as "*Gosekku* (五節句)". They are "*Jinjitsu* (人日)" on Jan. 7, "*Joushi* (上巳)" Mar. 3, "*Tango* (端午)" May 5, "*Shichiseki* (七夕)" Jul. 7 and "*Chouyou* (重陽)" Sept. 9. In those days, people were prone to get sick affected by the turn of the seasons.

On the morning of "*Jinjitsu no sekku* (人日の節句)", rice porridge called "*Nanakusa-gayu* (七草粥)" which contains seven kinds of spring herbs called "*Haru no nanakusa* (春の七草)" as shown above is eaten. "*Nanakusa-gayu*" is regarded as a kind of medicine that removes evil from your body and prevents any kind of disease. For it is believed that these spring herbs which endured cold winter must have survival power.

Eating "*Nanakusa-gayu*" on the day of "*Jinjitsu*" became popular in the *Edo* period.

"*Setsubun*" on February 3
(The last day of winter)

Oni

Roasted soybeans

"*Setsubun* (節分)" literally means the division of seasons derived from the old lunar calendar. However, today "*Setsubun*" means the day before the first day of spring only. It usually occurs around Feb. 3.

On this day, as a custom called "*Mame-maki* (豆まき)", we throw and scatter roasted soybeans inside and outside of our house while saying "In with *Fuku* (福: fortune)! Out with *Oni* (鬼: demon)!". The term "*Oni*" refers to an invisible evil spirit called "*Jaki* (邪気)" in Japanese.

After throwing the beans, we customarily eat roasted soybeans, one more soybean than our age, and pray for happiness throughout the year. The reason we roast soybeans is thought to block sprouting of the evil of the previous year in the soybean.

It becomes very popular to eat an "*Ehou-maki* (恵方巻)", a long *Sushi* roll, on the night, while facing silently toward "*Ehou* (恵方: the year's lucky direction)", and praying for health and prosperity. "*Ehou-maki*" should not be cut in order not to cut any good bonds in the future.

"*Joushi no Sekku*" on March 3
("*Hinamatsuri*" or Girl's festival)

Hinakazari

Clam soup

Shiro-zake **with a peach flower**

"*Joushi no sekku* (上巳の節句)" is an occasion to pray for young girl's healthy growth and happiness. "*Joushi no sekku*" was originally a ritual of getting rid of various stains by rubbing one's body with "*Katashiro* (形代: a paper doll)" and putting it on the river to float away, which is said to be the origin of "*Nagashi-bina* (流しびな)". And "*Nagashi-bina*" is said to be the origin of "*Hinamatsuri* (ひな祭り)".

Typical foods on "*Hinamatsuri*" are "*Hishi-mochi* (菱餅: pink, white, and green diamond-shaped rice cakes)", clam soup to pray for making a good match and "*Shiro-zake* (白酒: sweet white *Sake*)" with a peach flower which is believed to be the symbol of eternal youth.

Hishi-mochi

As pink color represents a peach flower, so does white color snow and green color a sprout under snow. They are respectively the symbol of eternal youth (pink), cleanness and the prosperity of descendants (white) and a charm to protect young girls from evil and to bring good health (green).

"*Tango no Sekku*" on May 5
("*Kodomo no hi*" or Boy's festival)

Helmet *Chimaki* *Kashiwa-mochi*

"*Tango no sekku* (端午の節句)" was renamed "*Kodomo no hi* (子どもの日: children's day)" in 1948, but both are still used. There is a custom that families with boys hoist the carp-shaped streamers called "*Koinobori* (鯉のぼり)" and/or display the armor or the helmet wishing their son's health and success.

We eat "*Chimaki* (粽: rice dumplings wrapped in bamboo leaves)" or "*Kashiwa-mochi* (柏餅: rice cakes wrapped in oak leaves)".

The tradition of eating "*Chimaki*" comes from China. The patriotic poet Qu Yuan (343BC-278BC) of the *Chu Dynasty* in the Warring States period drowned himself in a river on May 5. People threw "*Chimaki*" into the river to calm down his soul and tried to save his body from being eaten by fish. "*Chimaki*" is now familiar as a protective charm in Japan.

The tradition of eating "*Kashiwa-mochi*" was originated in Japan. "*Kashiwa-mochi*" is the symbol of the prosperity of descendants as "*Kashiwa*" leaves don't fall until the new sprouts come out.

"*Shichiseki no Sekku*" on July 7
("*Tanabata* festival")

Legend of "*Tanabata*"

"*Tanabata* festival" is derived from the legend of two stars, Vega and Altair. Vega, *Orihime* (織姫: a weaving girl), and Altair, *Kengyu* (牽牛: a cowherd boy), got married by order of The Load of Heaven. But they loved each other too much to carry out their duties. Then they were broken up by the Milky Way as a punishment. However, they were finally allowed to meet once a year on the night of Jul. 7.

"*Tanabata* (七夕) festival" is originated from the Chinese star festival called "*Kikkouden* (乞巧奠)", which was introduced to Japan in the *Nara* period. People wrote their wishes on the strips of five colored paper and hung them on bamboo branches in the night while praying that their wishes would come true. In the *Heian* period, "*Sakubei* (索餅)", one kind of "*Tougashi* (唐菓子: Chinese confectioneries made from wheat flour)", was believed to keep off malaria fever. And the court nobles introduced a habit of eating "*Sakubei*" at "*Tanabata* festival".

"*Sakubei*" is thought to be the origin of "*Soumen* (素麺: fine noodles)", which looks like the weaving yarn or Milky Way.

Nowadays we eat "*Soumen*" as an indispensable Japanese food on the occasion.

"Chouyou no Sekku" on September 9
(*"Kiku no sekku"*)

Kiku-zake

According to "*Inyou-shisou* (陰陽思想: a Chinese thought of dual cosmic forces, positive and negative)", odd numbers are regarded as positive numbers. As the number nine is the largest among them, the day of dual nine (重陽: *chouyou*), Sept. 9, was thought to have the maximum power.

"*Kiku* (菊: chrysanthemum)" was believed to have the power to get rid of evil spirits and to prevent diseases. "*Kiku no en* (菊の宴: the feast viewing chrysanthemums)" was held in the Imperial Court in the *Heian* period, and "*Kiku-zake* (菊酒: *Sake* with chrysanthemum bloom)" was tasted.

In addition, the custom called "*Kiku no kisewata* (菊の被せ綿)", rubbing bodies by the cotton covered on the chrysanthemum and wet with the evening dew, was performed by the court nobles to pray for their health.

Today, "*Chouyou no sekku* (重陽の節句)" is not so popular in Japan.

Kiku no kisewata

"Oomisoka" on December 31
(New Year's Eve)

Joya no kane *Kagami-mochi* *Shimekazari*

By the day before the New Year's Day, a major house cleaning is finished and the New Year's decorations such as "*Shimekazari* (注連飾り: a twisted straw rope with fern leaves, an orange and other items of good omen)" and "*Kagami-mochi* (鏡餅: round rice cakes)" are prepared to welcome "*Toshigami* (歳神: a *Shinto* God of the incoming year)". "*Shimekazari*" is the symbol of a sacred place and "*Kagami-mochi*" is an offering to "*Toshigami*".

On New Year's Eve, we eat "*Soba*" called "*Toshikoshi-soba* (年越し蕎麦: buckwheat noodles on New Year's Eve)" wishing for a slim but long and healthy life like "*Soba*".

Around midnight on New Year's Eve, the huge bells called "*Bonshou* (梵鐘)" are struck 108 times at Buddhist temples to get rid of earthy desires called "*Bonnou* (煩悩)". The sound of the bell is called "*Joya no kane* (除夜の鐘)". Each bell sound is believed to remove one of 108 desires of "*Bonnou*". Then, we are ready to greet the New Year by committing ourselves to making a fresh start in the upcoming year.

Arrangement of "*Washoku*"

Two Basic Principles of "*Washoku*"
~ "*Ichiju-Sansai*" and "*Gomi-Goshiki-Gohou*"~

Basic menu of "*Ichiju-Sansai*"

A typical Japanese meal consists of five dishes: boiled rice, soup (usually *Miso* soup), main dish and two side dishes. This is called the principle of "*Ichiju-Sansai* (一汁三菜)". Boiled rice is a staple food and a main energy source. Main dish mostly composed of fish, meat or eggs is a main source of protein which forms essential parts of organism of the body. Side dishes are usually composed of vegetables and provide the main source of vitamin, mineral and dietary fiber. Soup can work to supplement insufficient nutrients.

The other basic principle of a daily Japanese meal is called "*Gomi-Goshiki-Gohou* (五味・五色・五法: five tastes, five colors and five cooking methods)".

"*Gomi-Goshiki-Gohou*" together with "*Ichiju-Sansai*" provides a wide range of ingredients and menu and contributes to nutritionally well-balanced diet. The idea of "*Goshiki*" encourages us to take a variety of vegetables in the menu and makes the dish colorful.

Japanese meal is prepared to appeal to the five senses.

Expression of the Sense of Seasons

It is very important to exercise your sensibility to the nature and the seasonal changes to enjoy "*Washoku*". It is often said "*Washoku*" satisfies not only your tongue but also your eyes. The dishes are often garnished with inedible buds, leaves and/or twigs. The seasonal scent is also important. "*Kinome* (pepper herb)", "*Yuzu* (green or yellow citrus fruit)" or "*Myouga* (Japanese ginger)" can be served in the Japanese clear soup. They are called "*Suikuchi* (吸い口: fragrant garnish)".

A variety of plates and bowls of pottery, glass or lacquer also contribute to offering the sense of seasons. The choice of tableware shows the sense of beauty and hospitality of the cooks and hosts.

The use of chopsticks helps to enjoy such refined tableware. And to hold a bowl with your hands and to eat soup directly from the bowl are considered good manners in Japanese food culture. These manners are also a part of tasting Japanese cuisine.

Various Cutting Techniques with Kitchen Knives

Ume (Japanese apricot): carrot

Flower: lotus root

Leaf: cucumber

Leaf: pumpkin

Flower: *Shiitake* mushroom

Crane: taro

As many types of knives are used in cooking "*Washoku*", there are many Japanese cooking terms concerning cutting.

A variety of sophisticated cutting techniques contribute to pleasing your eyes in the Japanese cuisine. "*Kazarigiri* (飾り切り: decorative cutting)" is often used to cut pumpkin, *Shiitake* mushroom and lotus root as shown in the pictures above.

Another technique called "*Mentori* (面取り)" is to round off the corners of the ingredients to maintain their original shape by avoiding their loss while cooking. "*Kakushi-bouchou* (隠し包丁: hidden cut)" is one of the techniques for making food easier to cook or eat.

There are various purposes in the cutting techniques; to make food easy to cook and eat and to enhance visual and seasonal beauty of the dish and to supply us with pleasant food.

Foods add color to "*Washoku*"

Staple Food of "*Washoku*": Rice

Tanada *Ine*

Seeds of the gramineous plants such as "*Ine* (稲)", wheat, barley, "*Kibi* (黍: millet)", "*Awa* (粟: foxtail millet)" and "*Hie* (稗: Japanese barnyard millet)" have been served as important energy sources of the Japanese.

Among them, "*Ine*" has been especially treasured as a plant to produce rice, which is indispensable for us as a staple food. And Japanese people have used "*Inawara* (稲わら: rice straw)" as household goods without any waste. "*Inawara*" is used for various living goods such as ropes, "*Komedawara* (米俵: straw bag)", "*Mino* (蓑: straw raincoat)", "*Waraji* (草鞋: straw sandal)" and "*Shimenawa* (注連縄: Shinto twisted straw rope)". "*Momigara* (籾殻: rice husk)" is used for fertilizer and protective texture.

"*Nuka* (糠: rice bran)" produced when polishing brown rice is extracted to produce rice oil and used as "*Nukadoko* (糠床: bed of salted rice bran)" for "*Tsukemono* (*cf*. p.30)".

The Japanese have made various efforts to cultivate "*Ine*" and utilized the limited field of the mountainous country. A good example is "*Tanada* (棚田: terraced paddy-field)", which makes Japan famous for its traditionally beautiful scenery of the countryside.

"*Uruchimai* (うるち米: non-glutinous rice)" is mostly used as a staple food and "*Mochigome* (もち米: glutinous rice)" is used for making "*Mochi* (餅: rice cakes)", which is a must for various ritual occasions.

Leading Food of "*Washoku*": Fish

As Japan is surrounded by the sea, the Japanese have been traditionally blessed with rich fishery resources. And various kinds of fish have played a leading role in Japanese food culture.

In particular, the habit of eating raw fish as "*Sashimi* (刺身)" is a typical Japanese food culture.

Various kinds of fish caught in the best season called "*Shun* (旬: the best season)" are processed in many ways. "*Himono* (干物: dried fish)", "*Enzou* (塩蔵: preserving in salt)" and "*Nukazuke* (糠漬け: rice bran pickles)" can create new taste of fish. "*Narezushi* (なれずし: fermented fish in the rice with salt)" is a famous processed food in our traditional culture. "*Kamaboko* (蒲鉾: steamed fish paste)" is another kind of unique processed food.

Bonito is eaten not only as "*Tataki* (たたき: lightly roasted fish)" but as "*Namaribushi* (なまり節: boiled and half-dried bonito)" and "*Katsuobushi* (鰹節: dried fillet of bonito)". "*Katsuobushi*" made from smoked "*Namaribushi*" cured with mold is often used by shaving into thin flakes called "*Kezuribushi* (削り節)" to flavor other foods and as a base of Japanese soup "*Dashi* (出汁)" combined with "*Konbu* (昆布: dried giant kelp)" to bring out "*Umami* (旨味)" flavor.

Excellent Supporter of "*Washoku*": Vegetables

Kintoki-ninjin

One of the important features of "*Washoku*" is that it treasures the sense of four distinct seasons in Japan. As the range of the latitude is wide from north to south, the Japanese can enjoy various kinds of food depending on the change of the season.

In "*Hashiri* (走り: the beginning of the season)", we enjoy the coming of fresh taste of the season. In "*Shun* (旬: the best season)", we enjoy the best taste of the food in the season. And in "*Nagori* (名残り: around the end of the season)", we regret and enjoy the taste of the passing season while waiting for the next year to come.

Vegetables are always close to us and important ingredients that make us feel such change of seasons. But Japanese are getting less and less chance to feel the season by the vegetables due to the technical development of cultivation.

"*Takenoko* (筍: bamboo shoot)" in spring and "*Matsutake* mushroom (松茸)" in autumn are the typical vegetables that bring us the sense of the season. "*Kintoki-ninjin* (金時人参: an oriental varietal of carrot with beautiful crimson color)" makes us feel the coming of winter. It is one of the indispensable ingredients of "*Washoku*" in winter season.

Takenoko

Matsutake **mushroom**

Accent of *"Washoku"*: Soybean

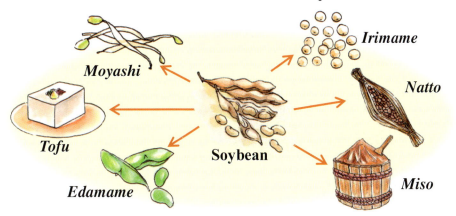

Soybeans are believed to be introduced from China more than 2000 years ago. The Japanese valued five kinds of grains called "*Gokoku* (五穀)", rice, wheat, "*Awa* (粟: foxtail millet)", "*Kibi* (黍: millet)" or "*Hie* (稗: Japanese barnyard millet)" and soybean. And we wish good harvest of these grains as "*Gokoku houjou* (五穀豊穣)" in the various seasonal festivals. Soybeans have played an indispensable role in the Japanese food culture among them.

Many varieties of processed foods are made from soybeans which enrich Japanese food culture. Soybean oil is made by squeezing raw soybeans. "*Kinako* (黄な粉)" is made by grinding "*Irimame* (炒り豆: the roasted soybean)". "*Go* (呉)" is made by grinding water-soaked soybeans. "*Tounyu* (豆乳: soy milk)" is made by squeezing "*Go*" after boiling and "*Okara* (おから)" is obtained as strained lees. And "*Yuba* (湯葉: soy milk skin)" and "*Tofu* (豆腐: soybean curd)" are made from soy milk. "*Kouya-tofu* (高野豆腐)" is made by freeze-drying "*Tofu*" as preserved food. "*Aburaage* (油揚げ)" is a fried "*Tofu*". "*Natto* (納豆)", "*Miso* (味噌: soybean paste)" and "*Shoyu* (醤油: soy sauce)" are made from the fermented soybeans. Young soybeans called "*Edamame* (枝豆)" and soybean sprouts called "*Moyashi* (もやし)" are very popular vegetables among us.

Accent of "*Washoku*": *Tsukemono*
(Japanese pickles)

"*Tsukemono* (漬物)" is an essential food for the Japanese dining. The merits of "*Tsukemono*" as a fermented food are recently appreciated again, though it had once been criticized for its high salt content.

"*Tsukemono*" was born as a method of preserving a lot of vegetables cultivated in the season. A basic method of making "*Tsukemono*" is to dry the vegetables first and salt them after dehydrating. During fermentation and aging, soft acidity and "*Umami* (旨味)" are added to them. The produced acidity inhibits bacterial growth.

There are so many varieties of "*Tsukemono*" throughout Japan and their characteristics are unique to every region.

"*Iburigakko* (いぶりがっこ)" in *Akita* Prefecture is a radish pickle with an added smoky flavor like a smoked food. "*Sunkizuke* (すんき漬け)" in the *Kiso* area of *Nagano* Prefecture is a pickle of red turnip leaves fermented without salt. "*Sugukizuke* (すぐき漬け)" is a delicious pickle with particular acidity given by unique *Lactobacillus brevis*, and is described as the cheese of field. "*Narazuke* (奈良漬け)" is a famous pickle preserved in "*Sake* (酒: rice wine)" lees. "*Nukazuke* (糠漬け)" is a seasonal vegetable pickle fermented in "*Nukadoko* (糠床: bed of salted rice bran)". In the past, every family used to have such "*Nukadoko*" based on their original home-made recipes.

Partner of "*Washoku*": *Cha*
(Japanese green tea)

It is assumed that "*Cha* (茶)" was introduced to Japan from China during the *Heian* period by Japanese envoys to *Tang Dynasty* China (遣唐使). "*Cha*" was very valuable at that time, and only limited people such as priests and aristocrats could drink.

"*Cha*" is unfermented tea produced by stopping the activation of the enzyme contained in the "*Cha*" leaves through steaming after picking them. The reason unfermented "*Cha*" has become popular in Japan is mainly due to the delicious softness of the Japanese water.

There are various kinds of "*Cha*". For example, "*Sencha* (煎茶)", the most popular among the Japanese, is processed tea from the sprouts of "*Cha*" plants grown without shutting out the sunlight. "*Gyokuro* (玉露)", the highest grade of "*Cha*", is made from the sprouts grown by shutting out the sunlight. "*Tencha* (碾茶)" is also grown by shutting out the sunlight and is processed to "*Matcha* (抹茶: powdered green tea)" by grinding with millstone called "*Chausu* (茶臼)".

By shutting out the sunlight while growing, *Theanine* content in "*Cha*" leaves keeps on increasing, which gives "*Cha*" deeper taste and flavor. *Catechin* contained in "*Cha*" has an antioxidative effect and more than one hundred kinds of aromatic compounds produce a relaxation effect. The thicker green tea served at *Sushi* restaurants called "*Agari* (あがり)" is expected to save us from food poisoning by the antibacterial action of *Catechin*.

Wagashi

In Japan, there were no "sweets" in the current sense before the arrival of "*Tougashi* (唐菓子: Chinese confectioneries made from wheat flour)" brought by Japanese envoys to *Tang Dynasty* China (遣唐使) in the *Nara* period. The word for sweets was written as "*Kashi* (果子)" meaning fruits. In the *Kamakura* and the *Muromachi* periods, the original form of "*Youkan* (羊羹: *Azuki*-bean jellies)" and "*Manju* (饅頭: buns stuffed with *Azuki*-bean paste)" were brought by the *Zen* priests who went to China to study. During the subsequent periods such as the *Sengoku* and the *Azuchi-momoyama*, "*Nanbangashi* (南蛮菓子)" like "*Kasutera* (カステラ: sponge cakes)" and "*Konpeitou* (金平糖: confetti)" were introduced by the Europeans. It is only after the beginning of the domestic sugar production in the early 18th century of the *Edo* period when such "*Wagashi* (和菓子)" was invented as those we have in the modern age.

Although there are a wide variety of "*Wagashi*", those of the highest grade like "*Nerikiri* (ねりきり: white bean paste with artistic coloring or shaping)" and "*Kinton* (きんとん: mashed bean paste with a seasonal element)" are called "*Jou-namagashi* (上生菓子)". These are classified as extremely sophisticated "*Wagashi*" and tasted in the tea ceremony. The sensitive transition of four seasons is expressed in the design and by the name of the confectionery called "*Mei* (銘)" which is a seasonal word just like "*Haiku* (俳句)". We appreciate firstly the design of "*Wagashi*" and then the imagination of the scenery living in our memory inspired by "*Mei*".

Sake

Description of "*Sake* (酒: rice wine)" appears in the topography named "*Harimanokuni-fudoki* (播磨国風土記)" in the early *Nara* period. During the *Heian* period, a variety of "*Sake*" was made by almost the same production method as the "*Sake*" today. It was commercialized in the *Edo* period. "*Sake*" called "*Omiki* (御神酒: sacred *Sake*)" has been used as an offering to *Shinto* God in various rituals. "*Sake*" called "*Katame no sakazuki* (固めの杯)" is served as a token of marriage-vow in the wedding ceremony.

The rice used for making "*Sake*" is specially brought up to be highly suitable for "*Sake*" brewing. And only the wick white part is used for brewing to eliminate any "*Zatsumi* (雑味: miscellaneous unpleasant tastes)". Fresh "*Sake*", unlike wine and whisky, is generally appreciated without aging in Japan.

It is no exaggeration to say that "*Washoku*" has been developed as an accompanying dish to enjoy "*Sake*".

Japan, as a country blessed with rich four seasons, has cherished the culture of appreciating the nature while drinking "*Sake*". We have such symbolic words as "*Hanami-zake* (花見酒: drink under cherry blossoms)" in spring, "*Tsukimi-zake* (月見酒: drink while moon-viewing)" in autumn and "*Yukimi-zake* (雪見酒: drink while enjoying a snowy landscape)" in winter.

Foods enhancing the taste of "*Washoku*"

Water

Japanese food culture has developed with the blessing of abundant water resources. There are various cooking methods to use much water like stewing, steaming, boiling and soaking in water in cooking Japanese dishes.

In addition, the quality of water in Japan is very high and delicious. Water hardness is generally defined by the content of calcium and magnesium per one liter of water. Japanese water is classified to soft water because mineral content is less than 100 mg/l. This is based on the geographical facts that Japan is not only located in Asia monsoon region but is a slim volcanic country. Much fallen rain on the mountains flows into the sea without staying in the soil for a long time.

Since it is easy for soft water to extract "*Umami* (旨味)" and scent from foods, Japanese basic soup stock called "*Dashi* (出汁)" can be made easily.

Soft water also helps us to enjoy the taste of "*Umami*" and scent of "*Cha* (茶: Japanese green tea)".

"*Wakamizu* (若水)" and "*Wakamizu-mukae* (若水迎え)":

"*Wakamizu-mukae*" is the first action to take water called "*Wakamizu*" from a well in the early morning of New Year's Day. "*Wakamizu*" is believed to have power to purge an invisible evil spirits called "*Jaki* (邪気)" of the year. "*Wakamizu*" is not only offered to "*Kamidana* (神棚: the household *Shinto* altar)" but used to make "*Zouni* (雑煮)".

Since the quality of water is one of the essential elements of Japanese cuisine, connoisseurship of water is required for the chefs.

Dashi

Umami

旨味

Monosodium Inosinate

Monosodium Glutamate

"*Dashi* (出汁)", Japanese basic soup stock, is essential for Japanese cuisine, which is generally made by extracting "*Umami* (旨味)" from "*Katsuobushi* (鰹節: dried fillet of bonito)", "*Konbu* (昆布: dried giant kelp)", "*Hoshi-shiitake* (干し椎茸: dried *Shiitake* mushroom)" and/or "*Iriko* (いりこ: boiled and dried tiny sardine)" etc..

"*Umami*" was firstly found by Japanese chemist, Dr. K. Ikeda, who discovered *Monosodium Glutamate* from "*Konbu*" in 1908. Dr. S. Kodama later discovered *Monosodium Inosinate* from "*Katsuobushi*" in 1913 and Dr. A. Kuninaka discovered *Monosodium Guanylate* from "*Hoshi-shiitake*" in 1960.

"*Umami*" is recognized internationally as one of the five basic tastes including sweetness, acidity, saltiness and bitterness after the discovery of the receptor of *Monosodium Glutamate* on the tongue in 2000.

As components of "*Umami*" have the synergistic interaction with each other, "*Dashi*" is generally made from the plural number of foods like "*Konbu*" and "*Katsuobushi*".

In the case of "*Shojin-ryori* (精進料理)", "*Dashi*" is made only from plant foods like "*Hoshi-shiitake*", "*Konbu*", soybean and/or "*Kanpyou* (干瓢: dried gourd shavings)" by avoiding animal foods.

It is said that the success of "*Washoku*" is determined by the flavor and quality of "*Dashi*".

Salt

Salt is an essential and main seasoning of "*Washoku*", and it is used in the various cooking processes as below.

1) A small amount of salt is added to "*Oshiruko* (おしるこ: sweet *Azuki*-bean soup)" in order to strengthen the sweetness.
2) A lot of salt called "*Keshou-jio* (化粧塩: makeup salt)" on easily-burnable portions such as a tail and fins is used to prevent these parts from burning with a flame.
3) When processing "*Udon*", salt added in wheat flour can promote a typical chewing texture of "*Udon*".
4) In order to soften the acidity of vinegar, salt is used effectively for the vinegared food.
5) Salt added in a boiled water can keep the boiled green vegetables fresh green.
6) A lot of salt is used effectively to preserve foods from rotting and helps to produce foods like "*Tsukemono* (漬物: Japanese pickles)" and "*Miso* (味噌: soybean paste)".

And salt has been used for purification ceremonies in Japan. Today, we see such customs as throwing salt to purify a *Sumo* ring before the start of the wrestling match and as the salt formed triangular pyramid called "*Morishio* (盛り塩)" beside the entrance of the restaurant to pray for good luck.

Miso and *Shoyu*

The origin of another name of "*Shoyu*", "*Shitaji*" comes from the meaning of the basic taste of Japanese soup, and "*Murasaki*" from its color (dark-purple).

"*Miso* (味噌: soybean paste)" and "*Shoyu* (醤油: soy sauce)" are important seasonings in Japanese food culture.

The origin of "*Shoyu*" can be traced back to sauce called "*Hishio* (醤)" from ancient China. Although there were already "*Kusabishio* (草醤: made from fermented fruits, vegetables, and seaweed)", "*Shishibishio* (魚醤: made from fish)" and "*Kokubishio* (穀醤: made from grain)" in Japan, the production of "*Hishio*" in full scale is thought to be started after the introduction of the recipe of "*Karabishio* (唐醤)" from China and "*Komabishio* (高麗醤)" from Korean Peninsula in the *Kohun* period, which resulted in "*Shoyu*" manufacturing.

In the *Kamakura* period, *Zen* monk brought back the method to make "*Kinzanji-miso* (金山寺味噌)" from *Sung Dynasty* China. And under the processing of "*Kinzanji-miso*", people in those days found out that they could use "*Tamari* (溜: dark sauce)" in the bottom of the barrel as seasoning. The Japanese characters of "*Shoyu*" was firstly observed in the book, "*Ekirinbon setsuyoushu* (易林本 節用集)", an early Japanese dictionary published in 1597.

Now, "*Usukuchi-shoyu* (薄口醤油: light soy sauce)" is popular in the *Kansai* region and "*Koikuchi-shoyu* (濃口醤油: dark soy sauce)" in the *Kanto* region.

Mirin

Unagi no kabayaki

Mirin

"*Mirin* (味醂)" is a type of rice wine with lower alcohol and higher sugar content. "*Mirin*" had been drunk as sweet liquor before the *Edo* period. And "*Mirin*" was used in various restaurants as seasoning. According to the "*Morisadamankou* (守貞漫稿)", the document of historical investigation written in the latter part of the *Edo* period, "*Mirin*" was used as the sauce for "*Unagi no kabayaki* (鰻の蒲焼: eel broiled with soy-based sauce)" and the "*Tsuyu* (つゆ: soup)" for "*Soba* (蕎麦: buckwheat noodles)".

In the cooking of "*Washoku*", "*Mirin*" is sometimes used as sweetener instead of sucrose. This is because the sweetness of "*Mirin*" is mainly due to glucose and maltose whose sweetness is softer than sucrose. In addition, "*Mirin*" contains various amino acids and peptides produced under the fermentation process, which can add "*Umami* (旨味)" to the dish. "*Mirin*" is sometimes used to give glossy effect on the surface of food as "*Teriyaki* (照り焼き)", which makes the food look bright and more delicious.

"*Otoso* (お屠蘇)" is a special drink on New Year's Day to wish for perfect health of the year, which is made by immersing "*Tososan* (屠蘇散: blend of several types of herbs)" in "*Mirin*".

Mirinboshi

~References~

【Heart of "*Washoku*"】

Heart of "*Omotenashi*"

http://www.pmaj.or.jp/online/1307/hitokoto.html (accessed Dec. 20, 2016)

Basic manners to enjoy "*Washoku*"

R. Minemura, "*Kodomo no* manner *zukan 2/ Shokuji no* manner", Kaisei-sha Ltd. (2000) ISBN: 4-03-406320-3

Heart of "*Shojin-ryori*"

S. Takanashi, "*Eiheiji no shojin-ryori*", Gakken Co., Ltd. (2010) ISBN: 4-05-402188-3

Kofukusan kenchou koukokuzenji, "*Katei de tsukureru meisatsu no aji/ Kamakura kenchouji no shojin-ryori*", Sekaibunka Publishing Inc. (2013) ISBN: 978-4-418-13334-5

Heart of "*Kaiseki-ryori*"

H. Tsutsui, "*Kaiseki no kenkyu – Wabi-cha no shokurei*", Tankosha Publishing (2002) ISBN: 4-473-01926-8

K. Ogura, et al., "*Nihon-ryori gyouji/shikitari daijiten jitsuyou-hen*", Prostar (2003) ISBN: 4-947536-32-2

K. Ito, "*Cha to zen*", Shunjusha Publishing Company (2004) ISBN: 4-393-14411-2

【Seasonal Events and Foods】

Editorial department of Houbunshorin, "*Kodomo ni tsutaetai nenju gyouji/kinenbi*", Houbunshorin (2012) ISBN: 4-89347-054-X

T. Shintani, "*Nihon no 'gyouji' to 'shoku' no shikitari*", Seishun Publishing Co., Ltd. (2007) ISBN: 4-413-04106-2

K. Ogura, et al., "*Nihon-ryori gyouji/shikitari daijiten yougo-hen*", Prostar (2003) ISBN: 4-947536-31-4

T. Kato, et al., "*Nenju gyouji daijiten*", *Yoshikawa-koubunkan* (2009) ISBN: 978-4-642-01443-4

http://jcolor.blog91.fc2.com/blog-entry-50.html (accessed Dec. 20, 2016)

【Arrangement of *"Washoku"*】

I. Kumakura, et al., Introduction to Japanese Cuisine: Nature, History and Culture, Shuhari Initiative Ltd. (2015) ISBN: 978-4-908325-00-7

【Foods add color to *"Washoku"*】

Accent of *"Washoku"*: Soybean

T. Watanabe, et al., *"Daizu shokuhin"*, Korin (1991) ISBN: 4-7712-9109-9

Accent of *"Washoku"*: *Tsukemono*

H. Iizuka, et al., "Kyoto *no kyoudo-ryori*", Dobunshoin (1988) ISBN: 4-8103-5034-7

http://www.kyuchan.co.jp/labs/tanbou/nagano/ (accessed Dec. 20, 2016)

Partner of *"Washoku"*: *Cha*

"Nihon-cha no jiten/ Irekata/tanoshimikata/bunka ga wakaru", Studio Tac Creative Co., Ltd. (2013) ISBN: 978-4-88393-558-1

Committee of *Nihon-cha kentei*, *"Nihon-cha no subete ga wakaru hon"*, Rural Culture Association Japan (2014) ISBN: 978-4-540-08187-3

Wagashi

H. Nakajima, *"Hito to tochi to rekishi o tazuneru/ Wagashi"*, Shibatashoten Co., Ltd. (2001) ISBN: 4-388-05882-3

Editorial department of Shinsei Publishing, *"Wagashi to Nihon-cha no kyoukasho"*, Shinsei Publishing Co., Ltd. (2009) ISBN: 978-4-405-09172-6

Sake

K. Sakaguchi, *"Nihon no sake-bunka/ Sakaguchi kinichiro sake-gaku shuusei* 1", Iwanami Shoten, Publishers. (1997) ISBN: 4-00-026186-X

http://www.japansake.or.jp/sake/know/what/01.html (accessed Dec. 20, 2016)

http://www.jinjahoncho.or.jp/iroha/otheriroha/shinzen/ (accessed Dec. 20, 2016)

【Foods enhancing the taste of *Washoku*】

Water

J. Hashimoto, "*Tsuudoku dekite yoku wakaru/ Mizu no kagaku*", Belet Publishing Co., Ltd. (2014) ISBN: 978-4-86064-404-8

K. Ogura, et al., "*Nihon-ryori gyouji/shikitari daijiten yougo-hen*", Prostar (2003) ISBN: 4-947536-31-4

Dashi

I. Kumakura, et al., "*Dashi toha nanika*", I & K Corporation (2014) ISBN: 978-4-87492-321-4

"*Dashi no kihon to Nihon-ryori/ Umami no moto o tokiakasu*", Shibatashoten Co., Ltd. (2006) ISBN: 978-4-388-06002-3

Salt

T. Hashimoto, "*Shio no jiten*", *Tokyodo-shuppan* (2009) ISBN: 978-4-490-10749-4

Miso and *Shoyu*

T. Kono, "*Choumiryou/ Shin shokuhin jiten 7*", *Shinju-shoin* (1991) ISBN: 4-88009-107-3

http://www.kikkoman.co.jp/soyworld/museum/history/index.html (accessed Dec. 20, 2016)

Mirin

T. Kono, "*Choumiryou/ Shin shokuhin jiten 7*", *Shinju-shoin* (1991) ISBN: 4-88009-107-3

http://www.honmirin.org/page/info.html (accessed Dec. 20, 2016)

K. Ogura, et al., "*Nihon-ryori gyouji/shikitari daijiten yougo-hen*", Prostar (2003) ISBN: 4-947536-31-4

Afterword

In the ancient times, it was very difficult for the Japanese to get their daily food and to spend a peaceful life. Japanese people believed that deities reside in everything connected with any events and everywhere. People expressed their gratitude or wishes for good harvest and happiness and paid respect to deities by offering foods and *Sake* at every opportunity throughout the year.

Now Japanese are enjoying the blessings of abundant delicious foods and healthy long life. To our regret, today's Japanese do not fully understand the meaning or wishes involved in the seasonal rituals and the food concerning the events.

This is one of the main reasons that we decided to make every effort to pass down the spirit and beauty of sophisticated process and form of the Japanese food culture to the younger generation through original educational programs. One of the fruits was the publication of the book "*Washoku no Sanpomichi*" in 2015. This English book is now published as an abridged version of the original text to introduce Japanese food culture to people in other countries.

We would be happy if this book could be of any help to understand Japanese food culture.

Study Group of Japanese Food Culture and Educational Program

Author and Editor:

    Kimiko Ohtani, Ph.D. (Prof. of Nara Women's University)

    Yukari Muramoto, Ph.D. (Asst. of Kyoto Prefectural University)

Author in alphabetical order:

    Jangmi Kang, Ph.D. (Assoc. Prof. of Hyogo NCC College)

    Machiko Yamashita, Ph.D. (Researcher of Research Institute for Culture, Energy and Life, Osakagas CO., LTD.)

    Motoko Matsui, Ph.D. (Prof. of Graduate School of Kyoto Prefectural University)

    Terumi Aiba, Ph.D. (Prof. of Kyoto Kacho University)

Illustration:

    Noriko Watanabe (Illustrator)

    Yoko Nakamoto (Student of Kyoto Prefectural University)

    Akiko Matsuo, Ph.D. (Graduate student of Graduate School of Kyoto Prefectural University)

    Students of Kyoto Prefectural University

Supervisor of English:

    Yoshihito Imai (President, iGbc office)

Finding *"Washoku"*
~ Japanese Food Culture ~

Editor:	Study Group of Japanese Food Culture and Educational Program
Author and Editor:	Kimiko Ohtani, Ph.D.
	Yukari Muramoto, Ph.D.
Publisher:	Hisaki TANAKA

Publishing office:
DENKISHOIN Co., Ltd.
Web Site: http://www.denkishoin.co.jp
Address: 2F, Miyata Bldg., 1-3, Kandajimbocho, Chiyoda-ku, Tokyo 101-0051, JAPAN
PHONE : +81-3-5259-9160 / FAX : +81-3-5259-9162

Ⓒ Kimiko Ohtani, Yukari Muramoto 2017

Finding "*Washoku*"
～ Japanese Food Culture ～

2017年 2月25日　第1版第1刷発行

編　者	Study Group of Japanese Food Culture and Educational Program
編著者	大谷　貴美子（おおたに　きみこ） 村元　由佳利（むらもと　ゆかり）
発行者	田中　久喜

発　行　所
株式会社　電気書院
ホームページ　www.denkishoin.co.jp
(振替口座　00190-5-18837)
〒101-0051　東京都千代田区神田神保町1-3ミヤタビル2F
電話(03)5259-9160／FAX(03)5259-9162

印刷　創栄図書印刷株式会社
Printed in Japan／ISBN978-4-485-30406-8　C0077

• 落丁・乱丁の際は、送料弊社負担にてお取り替えいたします。

JCOPY〈(社)出版者著作権管理機構　委託出版物〉

本書の無断複写(電子化含む)は著作権法上での例外を除き禁じられています。複写される場合は、そのつど事前に、(社)出版者著作権管理機構(電話:03-3513-6969, FAX:03-3513-6979, e-mail:info@jcopy.or.jp)の許諾を得てください。また本書を代行業者等の第三者に依頼してスキャンやデジタル化することは、たとえ個人や家庭内での利用であっても一切認められません。